The Iranian Protest Of Today

Brutality of the Iranian "Morality Police"

Arian M. Imad

Table of contents

INTRODUCTION

What's Happening In Iran?

Some women tore off their required headscarves during public rallies, spinning them in the air as a show of defiance. Two ladies were seen in viral videos tossing their hijabs into a bonfire. Another lady is seen protesting by publicly shaving off her hair.

At a few of the protests, demonstrators and police engaged in physical altercations, and Tehran's capital saw the rise of significant clouds of tear gas. The Basij on motorcycles also pursued protesters and attacked them with clubs.

In the past, demonstrations over issues like water rights and the faltering economy of the nation have been forcefully put down by the Basij, volunteers in Iran's paramilitary Revolutionary Guard.

Nevertheless, despite the potential of being arrested, imprisoned, or even given the death penalty, some protesters continue to cry "death to the dictator," directing their chants toward both Iran's theocracy and Supreme Leader Ayatollah Ali Khamenei.

The Cause Of Rage In Iran

The death of a young lady sparked long-simmering resentment.Mahsa Amini, better known as Jina, was detained last week while traveling to Tehran with her family from her home in the Kurdistan region of the country on suspicion of breaking the hijab legislation.

Numerous injuries have been recorded, and the protests have already extended to dozens more locations. Since the disturbance started last Saturday, the administration said that 17 people including two security personnel have died. Rights organizations claim that the death toll may be greater.

Large numbers of women have participated in the demonstrations, who originally went to the streets in uncommon acts of defiance of the government and its implementation of the nation's hijab legislation, which requires women to wear loose-fitting clothes and cover their hair.

The protests have extended, and the demands have expanded to reflect the ire of regular Iranians over their living circumstances as a result of years of U.S.-led economic sanctions, pervasive corruption, and economic mismanagement.

Amini was detained by Iran's morality police on September 13 as she was on a visit to Tehran from her birthplace in the country's western Kurdish region. She passed just three days after collapsing at a police station.

She was held by the police for wearing her headscarf too loosely. In public, Iranian women are required to cover their hair entirely with a headscarf. Now, only Afghanistan, which is ruled by the Taliban, actively executes legislation like that. Saudi Arabia, an extremely conservative country, has loosened its enforcement in recent years.

Police claim that Amini died of a heart attack and deny that she was treated unfairly. A probe has been promised by President Ebrahim Raisi, who addressed on Wednesday to the U.N. General Assembly.

Amini's family claims they were not allowed to view Amini's corpse before she was buried and that she had no history of heart problems. After her burial on Saturday in the Kurdish city of Saqez, protests broke out and swiftly extended to other regions of the nation, including Tehran.

Since the last wave of unrest in 2019, which was met with a fatal reaction, the demonstrations have emerged as one of the most prominent threats to the administration with remarkable spectacles of dissent and vows to overthrow the Islamic Republic.

The police responded once again with a ruthless and organized response, using batons and water cannons as well as firearms to attack protestors. The use of mobile devices and the internet has been severely restricted.

After the Islamic revolution, in 1981, the legislation went into force. It has long been contested by several Iranian women, and it is routinely broken all around the nation.

Ms. Amini, 22, passed away three days after being detained while in the care of the morality police, who uphold the stringent Islamic laws of the nation. According to a statement from Iran's security services, Ms. Amini suffered a heart attack in the detention facility where she was receiving hijab regulations instruction before passing out. According to press accounts, her relatives denied this assertion and said that she was in fine condition before being arrested.

Her passing swiftly touched a chord throughout the country and gave the public's long-simmering resentment of the religious regulations a human face.

The northeastern city of Mashhad is conservative and devout. In one widely shared video, a lady is shown shaving her head in front of a cheering throng in the southeast Iranian city of Kerman.

More Iranians have joined the protests as rage has spread across the nation, turning the situation into a vehicle for wider discontent with the regime.

Many Iranians, who have sometimes walked to the streets in recent years in protest, have reportedly found their patience worn thin by years of economic collapse.

How Are Women Treated In Iran

Iranian women are fully able to pursue their education, occupy public office, and work outside the house. However, they are compelled to dress modestly in public, which includes donning long, baggy robes and the hijab. Men and women who are single are not allowed to mix.

The morality police enforce the laws, which have been in place since the days after the Islamic Revolution in 1979. The Guidance Patrol, as the group is formally named, has positions spread out across public spaces. Both men and women are included in it.

Under the previous president, Hassan Rouhani, a relatively moderate who sometimes criticized the morality police for being excessively tough, enforcement was eased. 2017 saw the police chief declare that women will no longer be detained for failing to adhere to the dress code.

However, morals police seem to have been let loose under Raisi, a hardliner elected last year. According to the U.N. human rights office, young women have recently been forced into police cars, hit in the face with batons, and slapped.

How Has Iran Government Handled The Protests?

There are no indicators that the demonstrations will stop. The formidable Iranian security force, the Revolutionary Guards, said Thursday that the protests were sedition and that they needed to be put down to serve as a warning to others.

According to NetBlocks, an internet watchdog, and Iranian digital specialists, the government has considerably restricted the three major mobile internet service providers since the demonstrations began, severely interrupted the internet in protest locations, and banned websites like WhatsApp and Instagram. These sites have been heavily used by protesters to rally support and monitor the course of events.

According to some locals, Tehran's electricity was cut at night, leaving areas of the central and downtown districts where demonstrations had been more fervent in complete darkness.

Many enraged Iranians have turned their animosity against the supreme leader, Ayatollah Ali Khamenei, who sits at the center of the nation's political structure.

Death to the tyrant and "Death to the oppressor, whether it the shah or the supreme leader!" were shouted by demonstrators at Rasht, a city in the north.

The government has retaliated with a harsh and organized response, using strategies that have been used before in antigovernment upheavals. Social media is flooded with videos of protestors clashing with huge groups of riot police, who have fired at them with firearms and water cannons and beaten them with batons. Plainclothes Basij militia members have also been sent to suppress the demonstrations.

The Kurdistan Human Rights Network, which has posted names and pictures of fatalities online, estimates that at least 17 demonstrators have been murdered in the province of Kurdistan alone.

According to Hengaw, other rights organization, over 600 people have been detained and at least 733 people have been wounded across the Kurdish area.The location of the victims was not specified in the government's released statistics.

Iranian officials have pledged to look into the circumstances surrounding Amini's death while charging that unspecified foreign nations and exiled opposition organizations are exploiting it as justification to stir up unrest. In recent years, there has been a typical trend during demonstrations.

The governing clerics in Iran think that embracing Western practices weakens society and that the United States poses a danger to the Islamic Republic. Khamenei has taken it upon himself to characterize so-called "color" demonstrations taking place in Europe and abroad as foreign incursions rather than calls for more civil liberties.

Since US President Donald Trump withdrew from the 2015 nuclear agreement with Iran and reintroduced severe sanctions, tensions have risen significantly. For the last two years, the Biden administration has been collaborating with European friends to resurrect the agreement.

Nonproliferation specialists believe Iran has enough highly refined uranium for a nuclear weapon, should it decide to make one, and the talks seem to be at a standstill. The Islamic Republic maintains that its plan is nonviolent.

Without going into any detail, the governor of Tehran said on Wednesday that three foreign nationals had been detained during demonstrations in the capital. At least 25 individuals have been detained by Iranian security services, and the governor of the Kurdistan region claims—without going into detail—that three people have been murdered by armed groups in disturbances connected to the demonstrations.

Human rights organizations and activists have accused Iranian security forces of murdering demonstrators during subsequent rallies, including those in 2019 against fuel pricing.

Could the recent happenings lead to Iran's Fall?

Withstanding decades' worth of demonstrations, Iran's governing mullahs finally put an end to them by using force.The Green Movement, which arose after Iran's contested presidential election in 2009 and demanded extensive changes, posed the greatest significant threat to the mullahs' authority. Millions of Iranians flocked to the streets in support of the movement.

The Revolutionary Guard and the Basij militia launched waves of arrests as part of the government's violent crackdown in response. Leaders of the opposition were put under house arrest.

Neda Agha Soltan, a 27-year-old woman who rose to prominence in the protest movement after being shot and bleeding to death in a video watched by millions online, was one of the victims.

Victims from Iran's past "Morality Police"

The theocracy in charge of the Iranian government has always suppressed female protesters calling for more rights.

Since the hijab law's establishment in 1981, Iranian women have pushed the boundaries of what they could get away with. Younger generations of women became more confident as they matured, removing their head coverings in public and advocating for the repeal of the hijab law.

It is a part of a larger movement by Iranian women to change discriminatory laws and address problems including divorce, child custody, and the freedom to work and travel without the consent of a male guardian.

In 2017, Vida Movahed, a 31-year-old mother, stood atop a utility box in central Tehran, took off her headscarf, and waved it in front of the public with a stick. More women began to follow her example, which paved the way for the so-called Girls of Revolution Street demonstration, which the authorities subsequently put an end to.

This demonstration, which included her detention, is one of the most well-known ones in Iran against the country's mandatory veil laws.

According to Vida Movahed's attorney, Payam Derefshan, a court convicted Vida Movahed in March after finding her guilty of supporting public "corruption." November saw the arrest of Movahed. Derefshan stated she is on a pardon list, but the release processes are still in progress. Derefshan initially reported the judgment to the local media on Sunday.

Nothing formal was said. Pardons are periodically granted by the Supreme Leader, Ayatollah Ali Khamenei, and are often associated with festivals.

The public is often not allowed to see Iranian court procedures, and rulings are frequently kept secret.Iranian legislation mandates that women cover their hair and wear modest clothing in public. Those who break the law often get a fine of roughly $25 and a term of two months in jail or less.

Authorities have taken a more aggressive stance against the demonstrations, which they claim are a component of a campaign organized from outside by opposition organizations and social media platforms.

Sahar Khodayari, a 29-year-old woman who had broken into a men's soccer game, burned herself on fire after being apprehended. Following criticism from international soccer authorities, the Iranian government altered the rule to let women watch matches, but only in designated places.

Iranian football enthusiast Sahar Khodayari, often known as Blue Girl, lit herself on fire outside a court in Tehran on September 9 and later passed away in the hospital. After attempting to enter Azadi Stadium disguised as a male, she was punished with "appearing in public without a hijab" for disobeying the famed national prohibition on women entering sporting venues.

As word of Khodayari's passing traveled hundreds of kilometers away, a smartphone started to ping at an airport transit area. then ping. then ping.

The lady behind the @openStadiums Twitter account, who refused to be identified for security concerns, stated, "When I was traveling, this tragedy occurred."

"I was talking to the media and spreading the news in between my trips. I wrote and spoke with several journalists, but I had a limited amount of time and was often experiencing panic attacks".

"So many journalists contacted me through Twitter with requests to write about this tale, but they only wanted to focus on Sahar's fate. To find out what happened to her, they just needed to do a Google search. However, it's crucial to describe the motivation behind what she did in your writing. It wasn't an easy task".

The Open Stadiums movement has existed for about 15 years and characterizes itself on Twitter as "A movement of Iranian Women striving to remove prejudice & allow women attend stadiums."

A few female football supporters first staged a demonstration outside Azadi Stadium before an Iran vs. Bahrain World Cup qualifying game in 2005. Today, it has evolved into a campaign for women's rights in Iran more broadly and has become a debate point for the reaction of football's regulatory bodies to violations of human rights.

"Women began asserting this right as a woman's right in [the year] 2005. Because some other feminists were so against us, saying things like "In Iran, we have far more serious concerns for women's rights and this is nothing compared to them," it was challenging for us in several ways, according to Open Stadiums.

"I believe that one of the things we sought to demonstrate to them was that a woman has the right to enter any public areas, and we accomplished this since it is now a key priority of women's demand for their rights in Iran," the author said.

Open Stadiums demanded action to be made against Iran's human rights violations in letters to Fifa and the AFC before social media became widely used. They wrote to local and foreign news organizations to persuade someone to pay attention, but they mostly received quietly in return.

The international media didn't start paying attention until 2013 at the earliest. Sepp Blatter, the former president of Fifa, and Moya Dodd, a member of the executive committee, were traveling to Iran to meet with government representatives.

Moya was one of our stadium campaign's first backers, according to Open Stadiums.

In every place she visited, she brought up this issue. No human rights organizations were paying attention to our issue at the time. But once Moya brought it up, Human Rights Watch showed there and stood with us. Numerous additional human rights organizations and media from throughout the globe attended. She essentially made us much more linked to the world of football.

"I wanted them to know, when they were here on official business, that although half of this country wants to watch football, they are not allowed into stadiums. And Sepp Blatter brought it up during his meeting with Iranian authorities. At the time, it was a major issue.

However, Iran's government ignored Blatter's pleadings. Over the next several years, despite leadership changes in Iran and Fifa, not much progress was made on easing the stadium ban. Open Stadiums started using Twitter at that point.

"Twitter is quite significant. On the one hand, Twitter is very popular among young Iranians. On the other hand, even though a lot happens in Iran, few people outside of Iran are aware of it due to linguistic limitations. That was my motivation for writing 90% in English and disseminating information about this effort, according to Open Stadiums.

"Now, I can estimate that maybe 90% of women are aware of this prohibition, and even if they don't like football, they want this social barrier [removed]," she said.

Open Stadiums traveled to Russia for the 2018 World Cup with numerous additional activists, banners, and placards in tow. Every time the Iranian men's national team played, Open Stadiums was there to draw attention to it.

The passing of Blue Girl earlier that month thrust Open Stadiums back into the public eye.

The @openStadiums account received a ton of online support in the days after her passing from people, groups, and organizations expressing their grief and sorrow over the tragedy. A tweet from Khodayari's favorite team, Esteghlal FC, after which she is known, went viral.

I was thinking, 'A girl died, and I gained followers,' so I'm upset about that. It's a very terrible tale," remarked Open Stadiums.

"Even though I was miserable, I believe I must write about her. I hope that this tragedy leads to something positive and that justice is served. It is insufficient to just grieve someone.

Opening my feed was challenging since every post included a photo of Sahar. Her eyes are fixed on you. Everyone expressed their sorrow at this incident.

The Open Stadiums movement is concerned that Khodayari would once again fade from public awareness due to the nature of the current news cycle.

For other people, it's simply a cute picture when you see ladies dressing like men and going to stadiums, she said.

"However, a lot of these females were detained by the morality police, where they were sexually molested, made to strip nude, and had their privates examined. Many of them were younger than 18, and that was a really big thing.

"Fifa is to blame for Sahar's death and the difficulties we activists are facing. You should see the pressure Sahar experienced both during and after her incarceration. These significant issues are entirely the fault of Fifa and the AFC. The lives of others are in danger because of their inaction.

The Open Stadiums movement in Iran is about much more than just giving women access to football events. It has evolved over the last 14 years into a means for women to express their human rights once again and rebel against the restrictive ideas that have defined their lives. The global media have to keep reporting on their tales. It must not be in vain that Blue Girl died.

"If you visit Iran once and stroll through Tehran's streets, you'll see that ladies fight there. They battle for their rights every day. They are fighting against the hijab mandate. They are battling for everything, according to Open Stadiums, including the right to attend colleges and compete for employment.

You must be a warrior since there are many obstacles on your path. They want women to have children, stay home and cook, be wives, and do other things of this kind. However, the younger generation is outspoken and wants to assert their rights.

"And now, with the stadiums, it's kind of a symbol for women; if they can enter the stadiums, it signifies that they shatter one of the barriers in front of them. It will occur. No one can stop us".

On allegations of "colluding against the system" and "insulting" Ayatollah Khamenei, Nasrin Sotoudeh, a well-known Iranian attorney who represented women who removed their headscarves, was given a 38-year jail term and 148 lashes.

Iran's Nasrin Sotoudeh is a human rights attorney. Following the contested Iranian presidential elections in June 2009, she has defended political and opposition figures who are now in jail in Iran as well as those who have been given the death penalty for crimes they committed as kids. She has worked with Heshmat Tabarzadi, Shirin Ebadi, a recipient of the Nobel Peace Prize, and writer Isa Saharkhiz.

She has also defended women who were detained after appearing in public without wearing a headscarf, which is illegal in Iran. Nasrin, a 2020 documentary on Nasrin Sotoudeh's "ongoing fight for the rights of women, children, and minorities," was secretly shot in Iran. She was included among the 100 most influential people in the world by Time in 2021.

The nation hasn't witnessed protests this spectacular since the most extensive and deadly riots since the revolution began in November of 2019 in response to an increase in petrol prices. Lower-income persons were especially badly struck by the reforms and made up a large portion of those demonstrating in the streets.

Middle-class and university students spearheaded the last wave of demonstrations, the so-called Green Movement, which erupted throughout the nation in 2009. They took to the streets to protest the rigged re-election of the hardline president at the time, Mahmoud Ahmadinejad.

The Revolutionary Guards and the Basij were sent to arrest, beat, and murder protestors at that time as well. The government reacted severely.

Symbolizing the rebellion was Neda Agha-Soltan, a young lady who was shot and died.

Additional Economic Protests

Beijing - Human Rights Watch said today that since May 6, 2022, authorities in Iran have detained several well-known activists on bogus charges amid strikes by labor unions and continuous demonstrations over price hikes in dozens of small towns. Four labor rights advocates and a well-known sociologist are among those detained.

Without presenting any proof of a claimed violation, news sources linked to the intelligence apparatus have accused the jailed activists of interacting with dubious foreign players.

On May 11, the Intelligence Ministry announced the arrest of two European individuals who, according to the statement, met with teachers' union organizers and "planned to exploit the demands of unions and other organizations in society."

Arian M. Imad 35

According to Tara Sepehri Far, senior Iran researcher at Human Rights Watch, "the arrests of major Iranian civil society figures on spurious charges of hostile foreign influence are another desperate effort to muzzle support for burgeoning popular social movements in the nation." Iran's administration views social issues as inherent dangers rather than seeking assistance from civil society to understand and address them.

People have congregated to protest the announcement of increased prices for necessities in the coming months in at least 19 cities and towns since May 6, according to the Human Rights Activists News Agency (HRANA), an independent human rights monitoring organization. Two individuals were reportedly murdered during the demonstrations, according to parliamentarians. Unverified sources claim higher figures. These reports have not been verified by Human Rights Watch.

Anisha Assadollahi and Keyvan Mohtadi, two labor activists, were detained on May 9 during a search of their residence, according to HRANA. Reza Shahabi, a member of the organization's governing board, was detained by intelligence officials, according to a report from the Syndicate of Workers of Tehran and Suburbs Bus Company (SWTSBC) on May 12.

Reyhani Ansari, a different labor rights advocate, was also detained on the same day, according to HRANA. Without offering any proof, intelligence-related Telegram channels reported that Shahabi and Assadollahi were detained on the "accusation of conspiring with a foreign team trying to subvert" the government.

Saeed Madani, a controversial sociologist who had previously served five years in jail for his nonviolent advocacy, was detained on May 16 according to Mehr News Agency. He was accused of "meeting suspected foreign actors and relaying their working principles to organizations within the nation."

Madani was unable to leave the nation on January 4 to begin his fellowship program at Yale University because of restrictions placed on him by airport officials at Tehran's Imam Khomeini. Since then, the authorities have stopped him from leaving Iran and have repeatedly questioned him.

The two Europeans detained were identified in a video broadcast on May 17 by the Islamic Republic of Iran Broadcasting Television channel as Cecile Kohler, 37, and Chuck Paris, 69. According to reports, Kohler is a union representative for French teachers.

After the Coordinating Council of the Iranian Teachers Associations called for widespread demonstrations to demand changes to the pay scale system on May 1, the day before National Teachers' Day, the police detained scores of teachers union members during the final week of April.

The spokesman for the Iranian Teachers Trade Association (ITTA), Mohammad Habibi, as well as Rasoul Bodaghi, Jafar Ebrahimi, and other well-known ITTA members are among those who were detained and are still being held.

The country's main unions have increasingly been organizing rallies and strikes in Iran in reaction to the country's falling living standards during the last four years, and there have been several protests to press for economic demands.

To suppress famous dissidents and human rights advocates, security authorities have used disproportionate force, including fatal force, in response to these demonstrations. Thousands of protestors have also been detained. The government has not shown any interest in looking into significant abuses of human rights that took place under its watch.

Since the demonstrations began on May 6, the government has severely restricted internet access in several areas. Several films that have been shared on social media show the presence of security personnel and what seems to be the deployment of tear gas.

Three names of those allegedly slain during demonstrations in the provinces of Khuzistan, Chaharmahal, and Bakhtiari were made public by unofficial sources. The fatalities could not be verified by Human Rights Watch.

According to Sepehri Far, "Iranian authorities have long pushed to criminalize solidarity among members of civil society organizations both within and outside the nation." "The goal is to hinder civil society's oversight and responsibility of governmental acts."

The UN's involvement in Iran's Crisis

UN experts today harshly criticized the murder of Mahsa Amini, 22, who passed away in police custody after being arrested for allegedly disobeying Iran's stringent laws on women's attire by donning an "improper hijab."

The experts also condemned the brutality used by Iranian security forces in towns throughout the nation against demonstrators calling for justice for Amini's killing and human rights advocates. They pleaded with the Iranian government to refrain from using fatal force to enforce peaceful protests and to cease immediately.

"We are surprised and very grieved by Ms. Amini's passing. She is just another victim of Iran's long-standing persecution of women, systemic discrimination against them, and the imposition of discriminatory clothing laws that rob women of their right to bodily autonomy as well as their freedoms of speech, opinion, and belief, according to the experts.

Iran's morality police detained Amini on September 13 because they believed she was wearing an "improper hijab." According to reports, she was brutally abused by morality police officers when they transported her to the Vozara Detention Center following her detention.

Amini passed away on September 16 in a hospital after going into a coma in the detention facility. According to Iranian officials, she had a heart attack and passed away naturally. The experts noted that certain accounts indicated, however, that Amini's death was a consequence of claimed torture and cruel treatment.

According to the experts, "we vehemently condemn the use of physical violence against women and the denial of basic human dignity while implementing obligatory hijab regulations decreed by State authorities." "We demand that the Iranian authorities immediately launch an unbiased, independent inquiry into Ms. Amini's death, release the results to the public, and prosecute all responsible parties," the statement reads.

Since September 16, thousands of people in numerous cities, including Tehran, Ilam, Isfahan, Kermanshah, Mahabad, Saqez, Sanandaj, Sari, and Tabriz, have taken to the streets to call for accountability for Amini's death and to end violence and discrimination against women in Iran, particularly the requirement that women wear the burqa.

The experts said that Iranian security forces used disproportionate amounts of force against the nonviolent demonstrators, using birdshot and other metal pellets. There have reportedly been at least eight fatalities, including a mother and a 16-year-old girl, as well as many injuries and arrests.

Since September 19th, there have been reports of protracted internet outages in Tehran, the Kurdistan regions, and other areas of the nation. In Iran, there have been three significant internet outages in the last 12 months.

"Internet outages are often a part of a bigger attempt to suppress the Iranian population's freedom of speech and association and to put an end to current demonstrations. Under no circumstances can state-mandated internet outages be acceptable", the experts said, warning against a further escalation of the onslaught on civil society, human rights advocates, and nonviolent demonstrators.

The experts urged Iranian authorities to pay attention to the legitimate demands of women who want their fundamental human rights respected, saying "Over the past four decades, Iranian women have continued to peacefully protest against the compulsory hijab rules and the violations of their fundamental human rights."

As previously said, the experts emphasized that Iran "must remove all laws and policies that discriminate based on sex and gender, following international human rights norms."

According to Executive Order 13553, the United States is enforcing sanctions against Iran's Morality Police and senior security officials who have engaged in serious human rights abuses in response to these and other human rights violations there, including the violent repression of peaceful protests.

One of Iran's Law Enforcement Forces (LEF), the Morality Police, arrests women for wearing "inappropriate" hijabs and imposes various limitations on the right to free speech. Haj Ahmad Mirzaei and Mohammad Rostami Cheshmeh Gachi, both senior members of the Morality Police, are further designated by the Office of Foreign Assets Control (OFAC) of the Treasury Department.

Esmail Khatib, Iran's Minister of Intelligence, Manouchehr Amanollahi, the LEF's deputy commander, Qasem Rezaei, the commander of the Islamic Republic of Iran's Army Ground Forces, and Salar Abnoush, the deputy commander of the Basij, a paramilitary militia and a division of the Islamic Revolutionary Guard Corps, are also among those that OFAC is designating. All of these people have participated in the repression and murder of peaceful demonstrators.

The Iranian government must stop systematic discrimination against women and permit peaceful demonstrations. The United States will continue to express our support for Iranian human rights and hold those responsible accountable.

THE "MORALITY" POLICE'S DUTY IN IRAQ

The part of Iran's Law Enforcement Forces (LEF) known as the Morality Police is in charge of upholding the country's laws against immodesty and other social vices.

The Morality Police of Iran, who are led by Mohammad Rostami Cheshmeh Gachi, have shown a culture of brutality and overuse of force. Early in 2022, Rostami stated that Iranian women who choose not to wear a headscarf would face punishment from the Morality Police.

The Morality Police of Iran's Tehran division was led by Haj Ahmad Mirzaei during Amini's wrongful imprisonment and tragic death. According to E.O. 13553, Rostami and Mirzaei have been designated because they directly or indirectly behaved, or pretended to act, on behalf of Iran's LEF.

Senior security service representatives

Esmail Khatib is Iran's Minister of Intelligence and the director of the MOIS, one of the country's primary security agencies and a major perpetrator of grave human rights violations. Under his direction, the MOIS has taken harsh measures against a sizable number of advocates for human rights, women's rights, journalists, filmmakers, and members of religious minorities.

During his time in office, MOIS also actively pursued those who reported abuses and breaches of human rights in Iran, as well as their families and tortured prisoners in covert detention facilities.

Khatib is being designated following E.O. 13553 for having acted or purported to act for or on behalf of the MOIS and for being a representative of the Iranian government who is accountable for ordering, controlling, or otherwise directing the commission of serious human rights abuses against Iranian citizens or residents, or the relatives of those individuals, on or after June 1.

Treasury earlier designated Khatib on September 9, 2022, following cybersecurity laws for having directly or indirectly operated for or on behalf of the MOIS.

The deputy commander of the Basij, Salar Abnoush, has openly discussed his command-and-control duties over Basij soldiers during the demonstrations in November 2019. Numerous times, the Basij have been implicated in the murder of unarmed protesters.

In May 2020, Qasem Rezaei was chosen to serve as the LEF's deputy commander. Rezaei is liable for major human rights crimes carried out by the LEF under his direction as a senior LEF officer. Additionally, Rezaei personally oversaw acts of prisoner abuse including beatings and torture.

Following the lethal use of force on Iranian protesters, he defended the LEF's actions and urged further violence against demonstrators in May 2022. Rezaei, a former LEF border commander, was in charge of the brutal treatment of people near Iran's borders, including the use of direct fire.

Iran's Chaharmahal and Bakhtiari province's LEF commander is Manouchehr Amanollahi. During his leadership, the LEF put an end to demonstrations over food rationing in the province in 2021.

Multiple people were killed as LEF soldiers under Amanollahi's leadership used live ammunition on protesters to crush the demonstrations. Amanollahi was part of the

LEF's reaction to the widespread demonstrations in November 2019 that ended in the deaths of hundreds of protesters as a senior adviser to the LEF.

The commander of the Iranian Army's Ground Forces is Kiyumars Heidari. He has openly acknowledged his and his force's participation in the deadly crackdown on the demonstrations in November 2019 that resulted in at least hundreds of protestors dying.

According to E.O. 13553, Abnoush, Rezaei, Amanollahi, and Heidari are all being designated for being individuals working for the Iranian government (including paramilitary organization members) who are accountable for, complicit in, or in charge of ordering, controlling, or otherwise directing the commission of serious human rights abuses against Iranian citizens or residents, or the relatives of those individuals, on or after June 12, 2009.

Arian M. Imad 54

www.ingramcontent.com/pod-product-compliance
Ingram Content Group UK Ltd.
Pitfield, Milton Keynes, MK11 3LW, UK
UKHW022210200125
4187UKWH00038BA/1128

9 798354 348282